Emotional Intelligence:

Socially Awkward No More! How To Eliminate The Fear Of Being Judged By People

by Samuel Yildiz

Disclaimer

The information presented in this book is not intended to replace personalized, professional advice from suitably-qualified persons. In reading this book, the reader agrees that the author cannot be held liable for any outcomes arising from the implementation of the ideas or suggestions contained herein.

Contents

Chapter 1:

Introduction - Why You Need This Book

Do you often find yourself feeling inferior, anxious, or panicked in social situations? Do you fear being judged? Perhaps you feel bad in the breakroom at work because you aren't sure how to make small talk with your co-workers. Maybe you even feel as though you don't have much to say to your friends and family. Whether your problem is a general sense of awkwardness or a specific anxiety around communication, social awkwardness can make your life very difficult.

In extreme cases, social awkwardness can turn into full-blown social anxiety. People with social anxiety can feel so ill at ease in situations in which other people are present that their world shrinks as they lose confidence in their ability to relate positively to other people. Social awkwardness can mushroom from a minor problem that causes a limited degree of difficult at work into a full-blown monster that can result in panic attacks across various social situations. As a result, a vicious cycle develops in which social situations trigger anxiety, which in turn becomes a feeling associated with socializing. So how can you go about solving your problem and become less socially awkward?

Firstly, it's vital to realize that you are definitely not alone in facing this problem. Anxiety and depression are the two most common mental health issues faced by adults in developed countries, but social anxiety and milder variants on the same problem – which we'll call 'social awkwardness' in this book – are also frequently seen in the general population. They can affect anyone, regardless of age, sex, and background. In fact, you can bet that you know at least one person who struggles with these issues, even if they manage to hide it well from the rest of the world. People can become very skilled in concealing even quite serious problems from others. For example, a socially awkward person may claim that they prefer to eat lunch alone in order to focus on work but in reality this may just be an excuse by which they can avoid having to face their coworkers.

So if social awkwardness is so, well, awkward, then why do so many people feel this way? Well, a degree of caring what others think of us is not necessarily a bad thing. Imagine if no-one gave a damn about the opinions of their friends and family. How long do you think we would last as a society before war broke out? Here's a brief thought experiment: What would happen if everyone woke up one morning and no longer cared about their reputation or image? They'd quickly start telling rather too many truths, and would soon lose their close relationships.

Therefore, we need to strike a balance between caring a sufficient amount about our reputations and caring rather too much about what other people think. This book will provide you with several ways and approaches by which you can get it right. You don't have to perfect or eradicate all feelings of awkwardness – that isn't realistic anyway – just be willing to change and put in the work required.

However, before you get started, there's an important question that you need to answer. It's this: Do you want to get better? Are you actually ready to tackle your social awkwardness once and for all? This might sound like a rather silly question to ask. After all, there aren't any benefits of remaining socially awkward, right?

Yet it's important to consider whether or not you are really ready to change. Change can be, and often is, transformational and improves your life for the better but at the same time carries with it a great potential for risk. You may find, for instance, that if you change then friends and relatives who perceived you in a certain way (for example, as the 'shy one') have to re-evaluate their opinion of you, and this may cause them some discomfort. Therefore, you have to be prepared for the possibility that you will have to field some questions. In most cases, simply explaining that you are working on relating more positively to other people is enough to shut others down, but you may find that you encounter resistance from unexpected sources. We'll come back to this later.

Secondly, we can spend months, years or even decades building a self-image that reflects a certain set of beliefs we have about ourselves. This can make meaningful change very difficult. For instance, if you have believed yourself to be shy and socially awkward since school, then it's likely that you will have more difficulty in changing your thoughts and behaviours than if your shyness is a relatively recent part of your personality.

Make no mistake – you can change. People can make tremendous change even if they've been repeating the same patterns for years, and you can change too! However, it's important that you are realistic and fully anticipate the possibility that making such changes will be difficult. You may even wonder who you will be without your social awkwardness. The key is to take things slowly. Read the book through once without stopping. When you have finished, return to the beginning and then work your way through the chapters, implementing the lessons and exercises as they are presented.

Before we get started, here's an outline of what's to come. We'll start by taking a look at the origins of social awkwardness. Specifically, we'll look at why some people come to feel awkward in social situations on a regular basis, and how various factors such as childhood experiences, genetics, and the media can shape feelings and experiences. We'll also look at the role of panic and how we condition ourselves to feel in particular ways in certain situations.

Once you have gained an overview of the problem, you'll read about the skills you will need to overcome social awkwardness.

These include exposure, cognitive behavioural techniques, social skills and mindfulness. You will then follow a 12-day programme during which you will put these new skills into practice. Over the course of 12 days, you will stretch yourself by exposing yourself to new and difficult social situations. Finally, the last chapter looks at how to maintain a positive social circle and active social life.

Turn the page to begin learning about the origins of social awkwardness.

Chapter 2:

So Where Does Social Awkwardness Come From, Anyway?

The first step in overcoming your social awkwardness is learning where it comes from. Once you realize that it stems from a range of factors, you can start to feel a greater sense of control. Once you gain a sense of understanding and meaningful hope for future change, this provides strong groundwork for helping yourself.

Social Awkwardness – The Natural Side

As mentioned in the introduction to this book, a certain degree of social awkwardness is perfectly normal and healthy. For instance, if you were unthinkingly confident in every situation, this would not serve you well. It endears you to no-one when you act as though you know everything and never show your human side. Never make yourself feel bad just for caring what others think of you. After all, we wouldn't have evolved at all as a species if we didn't care what others thought of our appearances, habits, and so forth. It's only when this gets out of control does it become problematic.

Your next question may be this: At what point, exactly, does normal self-consciousness and the usual insecurities that come with human nature tip over into problematic social awkwardness? Put simply, it becomes a problem when it exerts a discernible and negative impact on your life or the lives of others close to you. For example, if you are finding it hard to function at work or find a partner because you are too socially awkward, this is clearly an instance in which it is negatively and significantly affecting your life. Or perhaps you are a parent who finds parent-teacher evenings very hard to the point at which you find it hard to talk to a teacher about your child's progress. Again, this is an example of social awkwardness getting out of hand. As a result of your problem, you may not be able to offer your child the support he or she needs. In addition, you could then run the risk of teaching avoidant behaviors to your offspring, thereby increasing the chances that they will also experience problems as adolescents and adults.

This isn't intended to make you feel bad for experiencing social awkwardness. But at the same time, it is important to realize that it can have a long-lasting effect on your life and that of others. See this as incentive to change rather than to beat yourself up!

So what, exactly, causes some people to be more awkward than others?

Genetics – You May Be Naturally Anxious

If you have suffered with social awkwardness and other anxiety-related problems for as long as you can remember, it may be that there is a genetic component to your issue. Think about your immediate family history, as this can also provide you with some clues. Do your siblings also suffer from anxiety? Do either of your parents – or even your grandparents – have a tendency towards a nervous disposition? Do they excel at the art of worrying?

The point isn't to blame your parents for making you socially awkward. Rather, the point is to underline the role that genetics can play in shaping personality and psychological issues. Research with identical and non-identical twins suggests that personality traits are significantly impacted by hereditary factors. Identical twins, when compared to non-identical twins, are far more likely to share traits and problems in common despite the fact that in general twins are reared in the same home, identical or not.

Note that these findings do not mean you cannot change! Research looking at the outcome of therapy and medication on even serious psychological disorders proves that people can and do change, and that it happens every day. However, it is still sensible to be aware of the fact that for some people, such change is more difficult than it is for others.

The Role Of Your Upbringing

Whilst genetics are undoubtedly a factor to be reckoned with, so are environmental influences. Psychologists have long recognized the role of parental modelling on their children's character and psychological issues.

A classic example of parental modelling relates to overly-anxious parents. For instance, let's say you were raised by a mother who had a tendency to be concerned about everything – let's say she worried about diseases, about the possibility of getting run over when crossing the street, about getting B grades instead of As, and so on. With a bit of thought, it should be obvious that this kind of experience sets children up to be anxious generally in later life.

In the case of social awkwardness and anxiety, growing up around a socially awkward or anxious parent can be enough to transmit some key attitudes to a child. If a parent is persistently negative about social interaction and about humanity in general, it will take a very resilient child to remain immune to their influence. It is more likely that such a child will be more skeptical than average of other people and their motives, and this may subsequently fuel their social awkwardness or reluctance to engage with other people in a constructive way.

Experiences As An Adult

Some people don't seem to have a family predisposition towards social awkwardness and were not raised in an environment that encouraged these sorts of problems, yet still find themselves feeling judged and ill at ease in social situations. Unfortunately, just because you have escaped childhood with no significant psychological or social issues doesn't mean that you can't develop them in adolescence or adulthood.

One common way in which social awkwardness can begin in adulthood is with a negative experience that triggers panic and is then generalized across other social situations. An example may make this clear.

Let's say that you seem to have no significant social problems until you hit your early twenties, and turn up on the first day of your first 'real job' straight out of college. You are eager to make a good impression and feel nervous, worried that you won't be able to meet the demands of the position. In fact, you are so nervous that you don't realize that the person sat at the desk next to you has been asking your name for the past couple of minutes. You feel silly, tongue-tied and self-conscious.

Now imagine that the next day, still feeling self-conscious and worried about creating a good impression, you are trying to make conversation with your new colleagues in the breakroom during lunchtime. Unfortunately, they don't seem especially friendly and you start to wonder whether you are ever going to make new friends at work and fit in.

Can you see how a vicious cycle might begin here? For some people, the above experiences can be the beginning of a general sense of worry and dread around social interaction in work or another specific situation as applicable. This can spiral into an all-encompassing sense of anxiety when it comes to dealing with other people. In such cases, a person can then develop a self-image as a 'shy' or 'socially anxious' individual. Psychological research suggests that we often live up to labels imposed upon us by ourselves or others, and this is why allowing yourself to be thought of as a particular kind of person is dangerous. Whilst is certainly possible to change at any stage in your life, it can be very hard to shake off an image. Start working on the issue as soon as possible!

Media And Society

It's easy to laugh at the idea of 'the media' influencing us and shaping our attitudes to social situations, but it's naïve to overlook the impact it has on our lives. From childhood, the average American watches several hours of television per day. Then there is the pervasive presence and influence of other forms of media such as magazines and websites that tell us in so many ways how we ought to look, act and behave.

From a young age, we are taught that in order to be successful, we need to be socially confident, assertive, and have lots of friends. This goes hand-in-hand with the messages we all receive about romantic relationships. Specifically, we are taught that in order to be considered a 'proper' adult, it's important to have a romantic relationship with a special person with whom we should be happy for the rest of our lives.

Thinking about it, most of us realize that such expectations are unrealistic. We know that very few people have the energy, time and luck needed to keep a wide social circle. Yet at the same time, we can too easily fall into the trap of comparing our lives with those of others. Celebrity culture also feeds into this phenomenon. It encourages us to inform the world of our every move via social media, and to compare our social lives with those of other people.

Social media can be especially toxic because you can too easily compare your 'insides' – the private struggles you face in your social and private life – with other peoples' 'outsides,' which is the public face they choose to present to others. Remember that many people are very selective about what they post to Facebook, Twitter, Instagram and so forth. There is so much pressure to present a life filled with interest, laughter and general positivity that you can easily be fooled into thinking that everyone is out there having a much better time than you.

If you are honest with yourself, you may find that the media has more of an influence on your mood and social confidence than you would like. There's nothing to be ashamed of in admitting this to yourself! Human beings have evolved to be highly social animals and it is only natural to care what others think of you. However, if you have been nodding your head whilst reading this section, consider embarking on a media detox. This doesn't mean that you need to give up all forms of media, just to become more selective about what you consume and what you post online. Start by paying attention to how you feel when you watch or read certain content, and think about cutting back on your consumption.

You could also stick a reminder somewhere near your computer screen – 'THIS ISN'T REALITY!' You could even make a wallpaper for your tablet, phone or laptop screen that gently reminds you that whatever you read on-screen isn't always an accurate summary of whatever is really going on in somebody's life.

Chapter 3:

Core Skills You Need - Rebuilding Your Self-esteem From The Ground Up

This is the longest section of this book, and with good reason – you are going to learn the skills and mental shifts required to fuel your self-esteem and dispel your social awkwardness for good! In this chapter, you will be provided with ways by which you can get to know yourself, develop emotional intelligence, revamp your social skills, and much more.

If you stop and think about it, most of what follows is really common sense. There should be nothing in here that truly surprises you. However, it's amazing how willing we are to overlook the obvious sometimes, especially if we have become stuck in a rut featuring the same set of maladaptive thoughts, patterns and behaviors.

There is a lot of information to take in here. Read the chapter through several times, making notes if necessary. There are several practical suggestions included too, and you should aim to attempt every exercise at least once. When it comes to improving your social life, practice is much more important compared with theory!

In Chapter 4, you will be given a list of challenges and tasks that will force you out of your comfort zone and make you engage with other people socially. In order to get the most out of the programme, you will need to make certain mental shifts and use particular skills. This is the focus of the following sections.

Small Talk – Not So Small After All

Do you roll your eyes when people try and make small talk? It's time to change your attitude! Although it can seem frightfully dull to chat about the weather or what your plans are for the weekend, when you begin to see small talk as the glue that binds people together, practicing it starts to make sense.

Small talk doesn't make you boring. It makes you someone who understands that a good way to start a friendship with someone else is to encounter them at a low level and not jump in immediately by asking difficult, overly-personal or significant questions. In fact, a decent small talk repertoire can get you through most situations, even if you know absolutely no-one in a room.

Stick to the basics. When meeting someone new, ask them how they are. Make a neutral observational comment about the room – a poster on the wall, for instance. Pass comment on the weather. It's a cliché for a reason – everyone has to deal with those pesky rain showers or sweats in the heat, so it provides everyone with common ground.

If you are attempting to make new connections with people in class, at work or in a volunteer situation, it's rarely a bad idea to ask them simple questions about their experience of that particular scenario. For instance, if you want to get to know your new colleague a bit better, start by asking them how long they have worked for the company. If you want to strike up a conversation with a classmate, try asking them whether they are finding the reading list for the term tough. It might feel as though you are 'boring' or sticking to tried and tested methods of making conversation, but other people actually appreciate those who put themselves forward and get everybody else talking.

It can be helpful to remind yourself that social awkwardness and anxiety are very common. Therefore, chances are that in the course of an average day, you will encounter several people who struggle to feel comfortable with other people. In such cases, your small talk has the power to do them a lot of good! By having a list of topics to hand, you are averting prolonged silences and providing a platform from which others can build.

Setting Goals

Most people picking up this book will probably have a general goal in mind – to 'become less socially awkward.' That's a noble aim, but it isn't really a goal. A true goal is specific, measurable, achievable, relevant and time-bound. It may sound odd to talk about goal-setting in the context of social skills, but it can work very well by giving solid structure to what can seem like the overwhelming challenge of changing the way you conduct yourself in day-to-day life.

To set goals as part of the process of overcoming social awkwardness, begin by picking a specific situation that causes you to feel anxious. For instance, you may feel intimidated on a social level by the weekly staff lunch at work. You may decide that your goal is to become more comfortable attending this function. That's a good starting point, but you would need to refine the goal further before you can start working on it.

To continue with the example above, a good next step is to identify exactly what it is about this scenario that triggers your feelings of anxiety. For instance, you might feel as though you never have anything to say to your colleagues when they ask how your week has been. A sensible goal may therefore be to think of ways you could respond to the questions they tend to ask you. You could even write out a list of potential responses in advance! It might seem a strange way to go about solving the problem, but spending just a few minutes mapping out what you could say may save you a lot of anguish in the moment.

Once you have decided what you are most likely to be asked and the ways in which you could reply, you could then set an additional goal to talk to a certain number of colleagues during lunch one week. In doing so, you have created a goal for yourself that is specific, measurable, achievable, relevant and time-bound. In other words, you know exactly what you are trying to do, how you are going to go about doing it, and how you will know that you have succeeded in your aims.

If you aren't sure where to begin when setting social goals, don't worry! This book will provide you with a good starting point. The 12-day programme given in the next chapter does much of the work for you, as it gives exact instructions as to what you ought to do.

Rediscovering Who You Are

If you tend to feel inferior to others in social contexts, this may point to an underlying problem with your self-esteem. In a nutshell, self-esteem is the ability to value yourself for who you are. It's an extremely valuable tool to have not only for life in general, but for being able to relate well to others.

When you value yourself, you have more confidence that what you say is worth listening to. This means that you will start to feel more at ease in social situations. So how exactly do you go about building up your self-esteem? It starts with a solid concept of who you are and what you stand for. When was the last time you sat down and really thought about your values, morals, and overall direction in life? What do you hold as most important? What are your most significant goals?

Once you have established this, the next step is to ensure that you are acting in accordance with your beliefs and concept of how you would like to be. The greater the congruence between how you would like to live your life and the way in which you actually live, the higher your self-esteem (and mood) will tend to be. Dedicating more time to particular activities will also allow you to come into contact with more people, give you more to talk about, and simply make you more interesting overall.

For example, if you feel strongly that a spiritual element is very important for a good life yet you don't find time to attend services, pray or meditate, your self-esteem will suffer. You need to take the time to carve out slots in your day or week for things that matter to you.

Living Mindfully

Over the past couple of decades, 'mindfulness' has emerged as a major buzzword and trend in popular psychology. Borrowed from Buddhist traditions, mindfulness essentially means being able live in the present, rather than focussing endlessly on the past or brooding about what may or may not happen in the future.

Why is this relevant to social awkwardness? Well, because much of what makes social awkwardness so difficult is the anticipation. When you are expecting to feel distress or be worried by social situations, this only amplifies your anxiety. This is turn can create more negative expectations, resulting in a negative spiral.

The cornerstone of mindful living is the ability to remain grounded in the present. Do this and you will be able to focus on what you are doing and saying rather than worrying about what others think of you. This will free your mind from so much of the worry that comes with over-analyzing the situation at hand.

To learn how to adopt a more mindful approach, start by incorporating a couple of mindfulness exercises into your daily life. Start by focusing your attention on a routine task such as brushing your teeth. Take a moment to notice what sensations arise. What can you see, smell, touch, taste and hear? When you notice your mind drifting, gently bring it back to the present.

Once you have successfully taught yourself how to pay attention in a meaningful fashion, start applying this habit to social situations. For instance, when you feel yourself becoming tense and panicky around others, bring your attention back to the décor on the walls, on the texture of your clothes against your skin, and other sources of sensory input. Doing so helps stop you from over-focusing on what other people are doing, saying and thinking. Concentrating on your breathing can also be very soothing.

Having Compassion For Others

A common problem people face when trying to overcome social awkwardness is the underlying sense of 'why bother'? The more cynical and misanthropic amongst us might be tempted to write people in general off as a waste of time and space, pointing out that us humans are pretty good at inflicting suffering upon one another. This kind of attitude isn't without basis in fact – it's definitely true that there are lots of unkind, rude, indifferent and hostile folk out there.

However, there are also a great number of people who possess many fine qualities and make excellent acquaintances, friends and partners. With the relentless bad news that surrounds us in the media, together with our natural human tendency to focus on what is difficult or negative rather than positive, it can be hard to remember this.

The following are two techniques by which you can improve your opinion of the human race generally. Why is this a worthwhile pursuit? Because research has shown that when we attempt to see others as basically decent people with whom we have more in common than we have differences, it becomes easier to sympathise with their struggles and to hold a more positive attitude towards them. You can see how this helps with social awkardness – when you feel that others are valuable and worthy of attention for their own sake, you become more motivated to overcome your own difficulties and make contact with them.

The first technique is to try and remember that everyone you meet is, as one philosopher put it, 'fighting some kind of battle.' We all have our problems. Even people you consider pretty abhorrent and barely worthy of oxygen struggle with some sort of issue or problem at some point in their lives. This doesn't mean that you should forgive everyone all their bad behaviors. You aren't expected to be a saint here! However, you will find that when you truly accept everyone around you as human beings with their own unique problems and lives, you become more accepting. You need to trust that even if you can't see these difficulties, they exist beneath the surface. Whenever someone irritates or annoys you, it can be calming to take a few moments to reflect on the fact that they are a vulnerable, complex human being just like you.

The second technique is to actively seek out examples of human beings acting in a positive fashion that benefits other people, animals, or even the environment. Google 'good news blogs,' or just make a point of searching for the good news on your friends' social media feeds, in newspapers, and on the websites you visit. If you can't find much to feel positive about, perhaps it's time to re-evaluate the media you consume and whose lives you follow. Teach yourself that the human species isn't all bad, and you will increase the amount of underlying positive regard that you have for everyone else.

Chapter 4:

The Power Of Practice – An Intensive 12-Day Programme

Now you've read about the origins of social awkwardness and the skills you need to learn in order to overcome it, the next step is to put all you have learned into practice. This is where the 12-day programme comes in. Follow these instructions and you will give yourself ample opportunity to implement everything that has been outlined in previous chapters.

All you have to do is take on the 12 challenges listed below. Don't alter the order in which they occur, because they've been deliberately set out in such a way that they range from initially fairly straightforward to quite difficult. The idea is simple – you undertake each challenge and use them as stepping stones to better self-esteem and social skills.

Day 1 – Smile At Five Strangers

The first challenge is simple – your job today is to make eye contact with, and smile at, five different strangers. For the sake of clarity, 'stranger' simply means anyone you have never seen before. It doesn't include neighbours or acquaintances!

If you struggle with severe social awkwardness, you may find this hard but it is an important first step to positive engagement with other people. A good way of ticking this goal off your list is to go for a walk in your local area and interact with at least five of your fellow walkers. It takes only seconds to make eye contact, give a brief smile and a nod, but it's a start!

Day 2 – Greet A Stranger

The second challenge simply requires you to do the same as on Day 1, but this time with the addition of speech! This challenge is a means by which you can become comfortable with the idea and reality of talking with new people.

Go for another walk. This time, say 'Hi there,' when you make eye contact and smile. You will probably find that most people are receptive to you and are friendly in return.

Day 3 – Make Small Talk With A Cashier

Do you usually complete your grocery shopping as quickly as possible with minimal social interaction? Do you tend to avoid eye contact with the store clerk, or make sure you always head for the self-service area?

Today, you are going to rethink your approach and actually have a brief conversation with a store employee! Pick up a couple of items and as the clerk is putting them through the til, say hello and ask them how they are. It doesn't matter whether they give you a response or not – the point is that you have practiced initiating non-essential communication with someone in a social context. You get bonus points if you've never seen that particular store employee before!

Day 4 – Phone A Relative You Haven't Spoken To In Ages

Today's challenge is designed to expose you to another kind of situation that can trigger social awkwardness and anxiety – talking to relatives that you don't see often. Choose someone you have a neutral or positive relationship with, and with whom you have not spoken for several weeks, months or even years. Most of us have a few relations that we kep meaning to call, but as the weeks roll by it never seems to happen. Well, today is your day to get it done!

If you like, jot down a few notes before picking up the phone. Ask them how they are, how their work or retirement is going, and enquire after their health. It doesn't have to be the most groundbreaking conversation ever shared by two members of the human race. It just has to be long and meaningful enough that you put your social skills into practice.

Day 5 – Phone A Friend You Haven't Spoken To In Ages

Day 5's challenge ups the stakes slightly. Whilst there is an underlying expectation and norm that families 'keep in touch,' this isn't the case with friends. Therefore, there is an added layer of vulnerability when you put yourself forward and reach out to a friend you haven't seen in a long time.

Again, it's fine if you want to make a few notes before dialling their number. Explain that you realized you hadn't heard from them in a while, and were wondering how they are. If you don't have any suitable friends you can call at this point, repeat the previous challenge or skip straight ahead to Day 6 and repeat it twice in a row.

Day 6 – Make Small Talk At Work Or College

Work situations can be hard for people prone to social awkwardness. Whilst we can choose our friends and to some extent our family – or at least, we can sometimes choose the relatives we spend time with – our colleagues are not negotiable. We have to learn to get along with them, suffer, or leave. It's a stark choice! The smart option, assuming you want or need the job, is to actively look for the best in everyone and learn to get along with them.

Today's task is to build positive relationships with your colleagues whilst practicing social skills and overcoming awkwardness. Make a point of initiating at least one non-essential conversation with at least one colleague about a topic other than work. Try and make it at least five minutes in duration. A reasonably safe starting point is to ask them whether they enjoyed their weekend (if you are talking to them on a Monday or Tuesday) or whether they have any plans lined up. Another opener is simply to ask whether they have had a good week so far.

If you are a student, then adapt the above suggestions for use with a classmate. In this case, you have more than enough in common for a simple conversation – you are both attending the same class and are presumably interested in similar subjects. If nothing else, at least you can ask them how their preparation for the upcoming test is going, or what they think of the course tutor.

Day 7 – Arrange To Meet Up With A Friend

Your next challenge is to proactively reach out and arrange a social meetup with a friend or acquaintance. This has to be arranged by phone, not merely WhatsApp or text message! Look in your diary, find out when you are free over the coming week, pick up the phone and suggest to a friend that you meet up for a drink, walk or other low-key activity. Then stick to your plan!

Day 8 – Seek Out More Like-Minded People

You are less likely to feel socially awkward around other people if you feel as though you have something in common with them. With this in mind, today's challenge is about encouraging you to meet new people with whom you have things in common.

Do some research and locate at least three groups, meetups or other means of connecting with people in real life that have at least one hobby or interest in common with you. For example, if you have a young dog, perhaps you might like to start attending a regular dog agility class. If you work from home as a freelancer, you could go online and find a local meetup group for people who are self-employed.

Of course you cannot expect to be friends with everyone you meet in such situations, but at least positioning yourself where others like you hang out greatly increases your chances of broadening your social circle. Don't be discouraged if it takes you a couple of attempts or attendances before you feel able to take an active part in conversations with others. The most important thing is that you try, that you take a positive attitude, and that you remain persistant.

Day 9 – Put Yourself Forward As A Volunteer

Day 9 is about connecting with your community, society and the world around you in a broader sense. Volunteering for a local event or charity is an excellent way not only to boost your self-esteem but also your confidence. When you give your time and efforts to a good cause, you prove to yourself that you are a worthwhile, proactive person who has much to offer the world. This has a positive knock-on effect, which includes increased social confidence.

Start by thinking about the kinds of causes and charities that have a particular meaning for you, and then use the internet to see what opportunities there are for people like you to help out. This will entail making initial contact with the organizers, explaining what you would like to do and why, and then of course turning up to help on a regular basis.

Volunteering really is an excellent way to gain new skills, find new friends and feel a tremendous sense of satisfaction as a result of knowing that you have contributed to a healthy local community.

Day 10 – Attend A Small Social Event

At this point, you need to move beyond one-on-one interactions and begin to practice handling group situations. Today you will be attending a gathering of at least four people and ensuring that you initiate conversation with at least three people.

So if you receive an invitation to attend a social event today, then go! If you don't happen to have the opportunity to accept such an invitation, go to a public course, support group or meetup group that appeals to you.

Day 11 – Attend A Large Social Event

Just as was the case on Day 10, a 'social event' does not necessarily have to mean a massive party, although you can feel rightfully proud if in your case it does! Today, attend an event for over 50 people. This can be a community meeting, forum or festival. Challenge yourself further by making eye contact with at least 20 strangers, and holding a conversation with as many as you can.

By this stage in the programme, you will have begun to realize that working through your social awkwardness opens up your world to a huge extent. You won't necessarily meet someone who could change your life at every event, but keep attending various meetups and gatherings and it is almost inevitable that you will forge new friends and connections.

Day 12 – Organize Your Own Social Event

Your final challenge will be significant – you are going to organize a social event for at least six people. This can be a dinner party, a coffee morning, a meetup related to a common hobby or interest, a BBQ, a birthday party, an outing to the theatre followed by dinner – you are only limited by your imagination here.

You might have to do some work in order to accommodate everyone's schedules. This is fine and normal! Just because someone can't make the first or second date you suggest doesn't mean that they don't want to see you. Remember that most people lead busy lives.

Planning will be absolutely key to minimizing your anxiety. Work out timing, food and activity details well in advance of sending out the invitations. However, at the same time, remember it is just as much your guests' role to engage with you and enjoy themselves as it is for you to organize the event and do your best to ensure that it all runs smoothly. To put it another way – this isn't all about you! Your role is to arrange an enjoyable gathering for people you like. Their job is to turn up, appreciate your hospitality and efforts, and have a good time.

Troubleshooting – What If It All Goes Wrong?

Looking over some of these challenges, you might feel very daunted. That's totally normal and even a positive – if these tasks were easy, there wouldn't be much point to doing them! You may also worry that you will be opening yourself up to rejection in some cases. For instance, you may worry what will happen if you invite a few friends over for dinner but no-one turns up. You may feel worried in advance about dealing with this kind of social rejection.

These are all valid fears – it is true that no-one could turn up, and it is true that you may have to try a few times before you find a mutually convenient day and time for everyone to attend. Yet this is an essential part of the process. It comes with learning to be a socially competent person who maintains realistic expectations about what they can expect from those around them. In the meantime, don't forget to keep working on yourself. Refer back to the previous sections on maintaining a positive self-image, good self-esteem, and a generally positive attitude. All these skills and qualities will not only make you more attractive to those around you, but they will enable you to see yourself as a worthy individual in your own right who is completely at ease in their own company.

Finally, think about the costs and benefits associated firstly with stretching yourself, but also in remaining in your current state. If you were content with being socially awkward and having a limited social life, you wouldn't have downloaded this book. You knew that something had to change, and change soon. There are immense costs associated with changing, namely in terms of anxiety and the necessity of venturing into the unknown. Your family and friends may also be briefly confused as to why you are acting in a new way. However, consider the cost of remaining in stasis. Do you really want to remain socially awkward for months and years to come?

Now look back over the steps and get started!

Chapter 5:

The Protective Power Of Friends - Building And Maintaining Your Social Circle

If you followed the 12-day programme, you will naturally have begun to increase the size of your social circle. You will have been in contact with a wide range of people and rediscovered your interests. This will make you a more confident, secure person who believes in their innate worth. Such an approach to life will make you more appealing to others, and you may have already noticed that people seem increasingly drawn to you.

Making positive connections like this is a vital part of overcoming social awkwardness if you are serious in your efforts to build more meaningful relationships with other people. You certainly don't have to be an extrovert or a social butterfly to be a social success, but the vast majority of us are wired in such a way that we feel the need for friends on a deep level. When this need isn't met, it can be easy to fall into a state of loneliness or even depression.

This means that maintaining friendships is an important skill to learn. Don't feel bad if this doesn't come naturally to you. There isn't a class on maintaining friendships at school (although imagine how different the world might be if it was made a core part of the curriculum!), and few of us receive explicit instructions from parents or other mentors. This means that most of us have to learn by trial and error, along with specialist resources such as books or even therapy.

What follows are a few guidelines for keeping your friendships strong. Think of them as the source of your social self-confidence, and an ongoing opportunity to become better at relating to people! Along with laughter during the good times and a source of emotional support when things go wrong, one of the best parts of friendship is the way in which it gives everyone involved a chance to learn how to relate well to other people. Therefore, keeping a healthy social circle is well worth the time and effort.

Much of what follows may seem obvious. Unfortunately, for those of us who have little experience in keeping friendships going over significant periods of time, some of the following information may be an important reminder! In essence, keeping your friendships strong comes down to being as accepting as possible – within reason.

Don't keep score

In a perfect world, everyone would give and take equally. Friendships would be built on a mutual, balanced sense of trust and respect. However, we live in the real world and such relationships are pretty much impossible to find! Why? Because we are all human, and we all make mistakes.

Even very good friends get on one another's nerves at times and say the wrong thing. It's even normal to have significant differences of opinion sometimes. For those of us who have been raised as 'people pleasers' who feel compelled to go along with what someone else thinks for the sake of keeping the peace, it can feel scary to assert yourself in your relationships. You may worry that when you expose yourself for what or who you really are, other people will reject you.

However, this vulnerability – putting forward your own opinions and feelings – is an important part of forming genuine connections. Think about it. How can you feel truly open with someone else and call them a close friend if you can't share your innermost thoughts and feelings? Here's another important point – if a friend is worth having, they will have the emotional maturity to understand that two people don't have to agree all the time.

Accept that they are your friend, not your clone

Sometimes your friends will make decisions that you simply cannot understand. Whether it's their choice of partner, occupation or lifestyle in general, they may well surprise and frustrate you. This is perfectly OK. All you have to do is remember and truly accept that the two of you are not clones – you are friends! No matter how well you think you know someone, they can still have the capacity to surprise you. Remember this, as it leads on to the next point...

Attempt to understand before you pass judgement

So your friend has done something you believe is objectively stupid? Resist the urge to lecture or harrass them, even if you feel it is for their own good. Think about times in your life when you've made decisions that perhaps were not the wisest. Did you want your friends to act in a judgemental fashion towards you? Probably not!

Instead, try to understand them rather than pass judgement. Ask them how they feel, and how exactly they came to reach the decision they made. If they are in a lot of distress, they hardly need you adding to it. Remember that the role of a friend isn't to make other people feel bad about themselves – it is to listen, to offer emotional support, and to help them make their own decisions.

This isn't to say that you need to blindly go along with every suggestion your friends make. If they seem on the verge of doing something really stupid, by all means point out the reason why a particular course of action isn't a wise idea. Just remind yourself that your primary role is to listen to their account of their own life and validate their feelings. You are not a psychiatrist, lawyer or therapist, so resist the urge to act like one! Always attempt to find some common ground between your experiences.

Be the first to reach out

These days, we all lead busy lives. The pace of change seems to be ever accelerating, and lots of us suffer information and commitment overload. Whilst there are more opportunities than ever before and means of organizing our social lives, it can be harder to find the time to reach out to friends.

Another factor contributing to this problem is proximity. Just a few decades ago, most people would stay in just one or two places for the duration of their lifetimes. They would typically meet and marry someone local, and work for the same company or in the same profession for many years. Not having the internet, people focused their attention on people close to them. This meant that everyone knew everyone else, and members of the community monitored one another's behaviors. Whilst this had downsides – the number of potential dating partners was very limited in some areas, for instance – at least most people had a readymade social circle.

With the advent of the internet and increased social mobility, it has become increasingly normal and even expected for people to move away from their place of birth. This has its upsides, but does mean that friendship groups become fragmented. Despite the availability of social media, posting Facebook messages isn't adequate compensation for actually spending time with your friends in person. Don't be afraid to be the first to reach out, even if it's been you making the first move for the last couple of occasions. Your true friends won't mind at all. In fact, they will be grateful. Being the instigator doesn't make you needy or desperate, it means that you value your friendships and are willing to make the effort needed to keep the bonds intact.

Don't take your friends for granted

If you have been friends with someone for many years, you can start to always assume that they will be there for you and even to take them for granted. Whilst it's nice to feel as though your friends will be there when you need someone to talk to or someone to spend time with, you risk alienating or annoying them when you start to assume they will be forever willing to prop you up in life.

Make sure that you take the time to say 'Thank you' to the people who are there for you on a regular basis. It's always better to err on the side of saying 'Thank you' too often rather than not often enough! If your friends have been there for you during an especially trying time in your life, why not thank them by taking them out for lunch or giving them each a small gift? You don't have to spend a lot of time and money in showing that you care about and appreciate them, and they will feel touched that you have made the effort.

Situations and people change, and it's unlikely that the friends you have today will be the same ones you have in a decade's time. Illness, relocation and other factors all conspire to keep social circles changing. This isn't to say that you should constantly be anticipating that your friends will leave you. Rather, there are two lessons to be taken from this simple truth. Firstly, you should try to appreciate what you have in the present. Secondly, it's always a good idea to keep on expanding your social circle whenever possible. Of course you don't want to overbook yourself or just make friends for the sake of it, but it's smart to keep your social skills sharp and mind broad by exposing yourself to a variety of different people. Keep curious and keep busy, and new friends will find you!

Don't confuse virtual friends with real-life friends

Nowadays it's easy to go online and get talking to people any time of the day or night. Whether via dating apps, message boards or comments sections on websites, you can find yourself feeling a strong sense of intimacy towards someone you have only known a short time, and have never actually met.

In this kind of situation, you must take care not to fall into the trap of assuming that just because you have swapped intimate stories or information with a stranger – even if they seem attractive, kind and smart – that you have become friends. This is true even if you talk on an ongoing basis. To really count someone as a friend, you must be able to share in everyday, real life experiences together. This means being able to get on well in person, where you don't have the option to press 'Delete' and edit the messages you send one another.

This is not to say that people who meet online cannot become friends. Rather, it's a cautionery note – if you meet someone with whom you feel a great connection, aim to meet them in person as soon as possible to ascertain whether you can really see yourselves becoming friends. Sometimes it is impossible to 'read' someone via text-based messages or video chat. Don't waste valuable time and energy on relating to a computer or phone screen when you could be out meeting people who can actually shake your hand and talk face-to-face.

This is a particular temptation for those with social awkwardness and anxiety. Online folk can feel a lot less threatening than real flesh-and-blood people you may meet out there in the real world. Online, you can always press 'Exit' on a chatroom, or simply choose not to respond to a message. As a result, you can feel safe and rarely overwhelmed. The problem is, though, that you need to practice your social skills in the real world! Shut off from the computer and get yourself outside.

A final note on the topic pertains to personal safety. Although there are plenty of dodgy people out there in the real world, it is particularly easy to prey on vulnerable, lonely people online. As soon as anyone gives you odd or suspicious feelings, move on. It doesn't matter how long you have been talking – you don't owe an online person, who will always be a kind of stranger until you meet and get to know them in real life, any explanation. There is no reason to feel guilty about blocking and avoiding someone who just doesn't make you feel quite right.

Know when to fold

As valuable as friendship is, it's also important to be aware when it's time to reduce or even cut contact with someone. As you become more socially skilled and meet more people, you will have to make decisions concerning who is most worthy of your time. If you have been in the habit of trying to get everyone to like and accept you, this may be an alien concept. Put simply, whilst you have to put effort to get the kinds of friendships you want, there are certain types of people who won't add anything to the quality of your life.

Spotting and dealingw with toxic people is a topic worthy of a book in its own right, but the essential point is this: If you have a 'friend' who tends to lower your mood and energy levels whenever you spend time with them, this is a person you need to consider removing from your life. There is no law that states once you are friends with someone, you must remain so with them for as long as you both shall live. It is perfectly OK to come to the realization that a particular person just isn't right for you.

If you find yourself in this situation, the best approach is to be subtle. Gradually withdraw communication. Most people should be able to take a hint in such a scenario. However, if they explicitly ask you why you have decreased your level of contact, it's best to be honest and say that you don't feel as though the friendship is adding much to your life and that you feel it is best to spend some time apart.

Know when to get help

If, despite following the above programme and working on your social skills you still find yourself frequently worried and troubled with regards to friendships and other relationships, it may be time to seek help from a suitably-qualified professional. For instance, a therapist may be able to assist you in developing more positive attitudes and behaviours that will help you build a social circle.

Ask your usual healthcare provider for recommendations, or contact a local mental health charity for assistance. The most important predictor of whether a therapeutic intervention will be successful is the relationship between client and counsellor. This means that you shouldn't be afraid to try another therapist if the first doesn't feel quite right for you. You need to be able to trust the person with whom you are working. You should feel confident that they are suitably-qualified, that they have experience in working with your problem, and that they have your best interests at heart. This doesn't mean that a good therapist should never challenge you. However, they should be willing to point out inconsistencies in your thought processes and gently guide you to a position in which you can re-assess your life and make positive headway towards a new way of being.

There is absolutely nothing wrong with seeking this kind of help. It is not a sign of weakness. On the contrary, it is actually a sign of great self-awareness and strength when you can take an honest look at yourself, identify your own weak areas and decide to proactively seek out the help you need to work on yourself.

Conclusion

Thank you for downloading and reading this book! Now that you know where social awkwardness comes from and are equipped with penty of ways in which to deal with it, you can start to look forward to a happier life in which interacting with other people causes you less distress and more pleasure.

Remember that change is certainly possible, but it seldom happens overnight. Don't be discouraged – practice makes perfect, so stick with the programme and forgive yourself if things don't quite work out as you would like. Dust yourself off, get back up, and try again!

If you have found this book helpful, please consider leaving a review for other people to read.

Good luck!

www.ingramcontent.com/pod-product-compliance
Lightning Source LLC
Chambersburg PA
CBHW030548290526
45786CB00004B/1927